GIAN CARLO
MENOTTI

Ricercare

for
Organ

G. SCHIRMER, Inc.

DISTRIBUTED BY

HAL•LEONARD™
CORPORATION
7777 W. BLUEMOUND RD. P.O. BOX 13819 MILWAUKEE, WI 53213

RICERCARE

Gian Carlo Menotti
(1984)

4

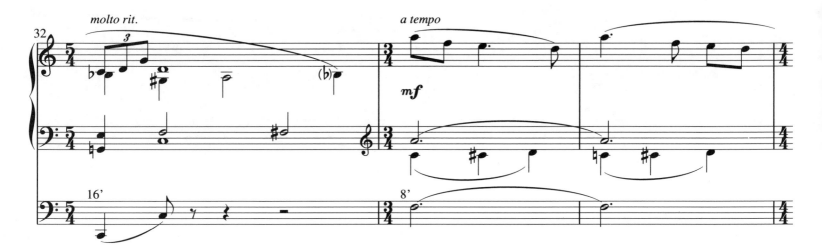

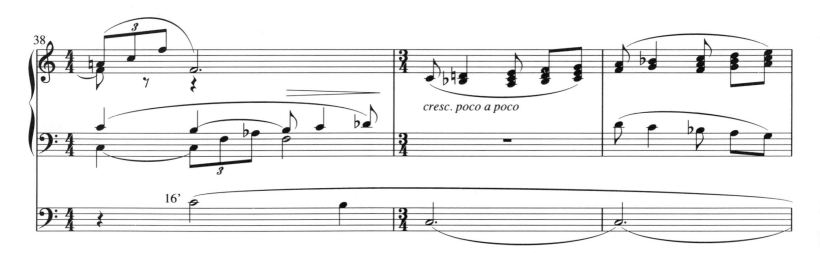

Poco più mosso, ma senza correre,
el sempre espressivo

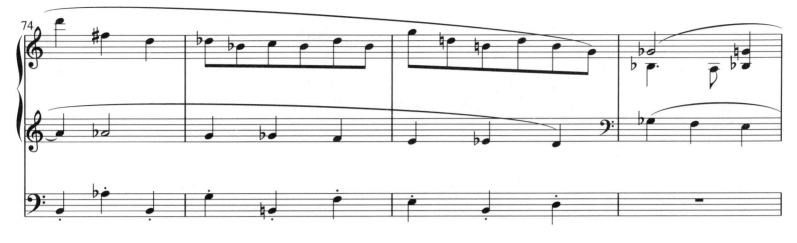

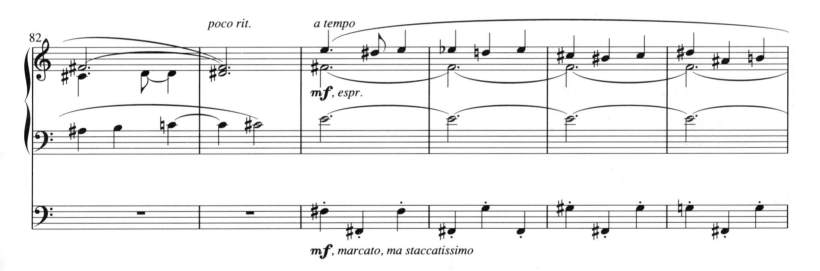

Allegro scherzoso

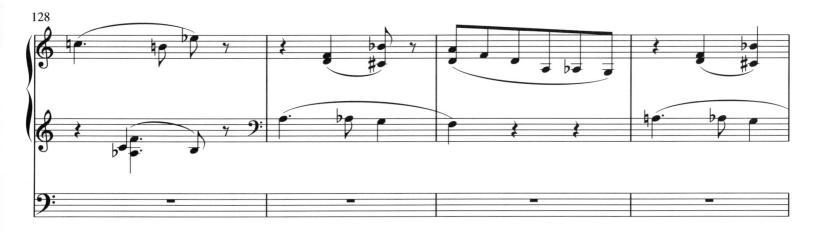

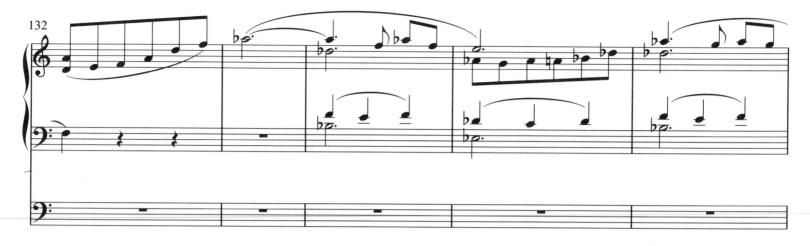

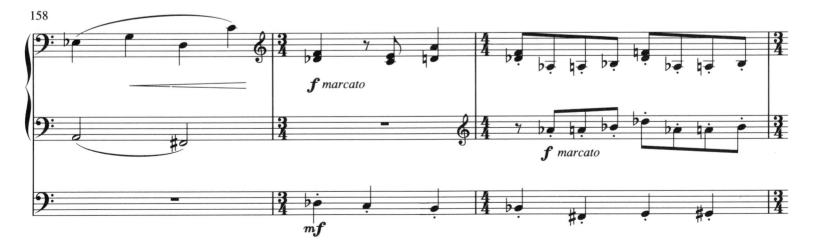

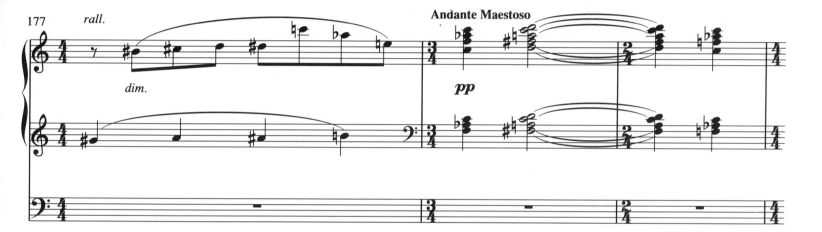

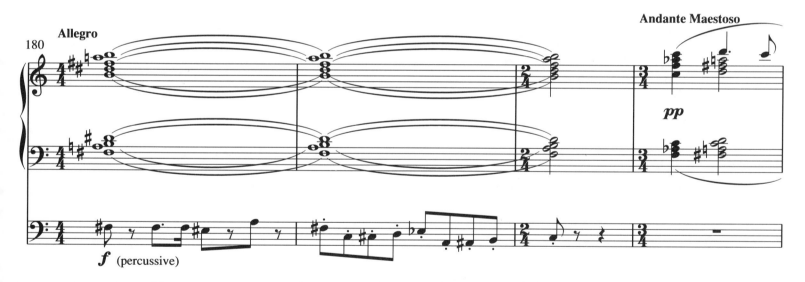

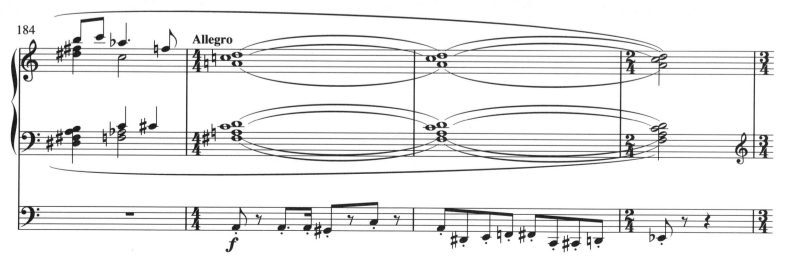

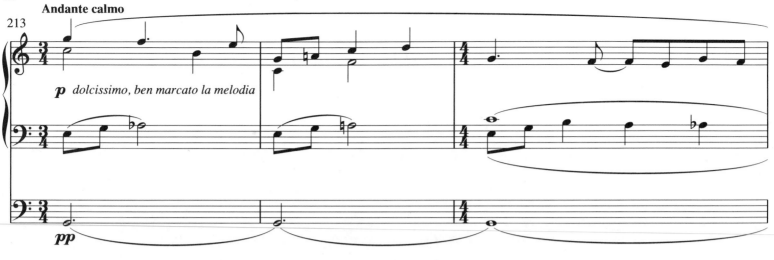